Journeys to [illegible]

A Gentle Guide to Mindfulness Meditation

Elizabeth English

MUD PIE

Mud Pie Books

Oxford OX2 6HY
Registered Co. No. 4405635

ISBN 978-1-912952-06-9

www.mudpiebooks.com

MUD
PIE

For my father, as promised
(1934–2018)

Let me be your mirror

Let me be your mirror, all the same,
To show another image shining back;
Comb out the matted tangles and the shame,
And see again the gold you think you lack;
In this reflection, all you are is here,
But bathed in gentleness, a different light,
Which brushes you with kindness, says to fear:
There's nothing here to turn from, or to fight.
Stand here now naked only to yourself,
And love your body, see how it enfolds
You, with every crease and crinkle, you by stealth,
You, defined by all that your heart holds.
    Don't ask me now which mirror is more real,
    Look deep in both – and tell me what you feel.

Contents

On Meditation

A word before we begin, on the word itself: meditation.

It means so many things. People say: *I meditate when I walk the dogs*, or *Music is my meditation*, or *Meditating means gazing out the window*. Others chant or follow meditations from one religious tradition or another. Others still practise secular mindfulness techniques, or listen to recordings or relax in a yoga class. Some people sit, some walk, some lie down. Some say: *Meditation is a useful word to hide the fact I'm nodding off.*

For myself, it's all of these at different times. What I mean by meditation is: *Whatever you do when you say you are meditating*. The most useful definition is probably your own. You discover for yourself what helps or heals. 'Healing,' after all, was what meditation originally meant (from the Latin, *meditari*).

The words in this book are offered to enrich *whatever* happens when you sit down with yourself and the world for company. And if a God or gods, spirits, saints or bodhisattvas are part of your world – although I rarely mention them here – they are welcome too.

Foreword

Poems are meant to slow us down. Often, we read and listen in a way that's uncomfortably like eating fast food – we stuff it in so as to fill a gap and guarantee that we keep going. We don't stop and savour, we don't let ourselves feel surprise or wonder or strangeness. And just as a diet of fast food is not much good in the long run for a well-functioning body, so rapid, business-like, 'practical' language leaves us that bit less human, less alive. A poem invites us to listen harder to words and sense their mobility, their inner richness, the puzzlement and enlargement they can offer. It takes a moment, or a connection between perceptions or sounds, or a single odd and arresting picture and says, in effect, 'Take your time with this; let it be and sit with it. Don't look for a "message" or a bright idea; just give time for your mind and heart to be opened up to find a little more space in the world.'

Of course, poems can be startling and shocking, they can be difficult, even painful to read. The challenge to stop and listen may mean being asked to listen to things we'd rather not hear in ourselves or in the world around (this is what great tragic dramas do for us). But the point is to give time. Sitting with a poem is often a way of stopping ourselves rushing off to another bit of busy surface activity that blocks up the deeper springs of insight and action. We sit with it until it begins to 'deliver' something – not a new theory or plan, simply that sense of a larger world, which may be more beautiful or more alarming than we expected, or both.

Many poems, then, are a very good accompaniment to meditation – a preparation for it that eases us out of our normal feverish activity, and an articulation of some of what meditation gives us. One of the great mystics of the Christian Church, Teresa of Avila, noticed hundreds of years ago that meditation gave rise to poetry; and her friend and guide, John of the Cross, embodied his most important teachings in poems as well as prose treatises. It was the Zen Buddhist tradition that shaped the form of the *haiku* which seeks to 'hold' a moment of simple transparent perception in a few lines of poetry. And whether or not you share any traditional religious affiliation, the act of sitting in still and non-anxious self-awareness is closely linked with whatever it is that generates the kind of poetry that washes and refreshes our gaze on the world. In this book, Elizabeth shows us beautifully how the words of a poem can grow out of and lead into meditative awareness, how they can nudge you gently towards a fresh and deeper resource for understanding, and for knowing and loving the fragile whatever-it-is that sits and waits and grows.

This is a book of real wisdom and grace; a travelling companion for the work that is done in silence, far below the surface of the mind.

Rowan Williams

Preface

Here I am – it must be twenty years back – meditating in my room. The room is peaceful, but I am not. In my mind's eye I'm seeing terrifying images – disasters from news reports, awful stories of untimely death. They arrive, unasked for and unwanted. My breath catches in my body and I flinch. So I summon all I've learned. I draw on years of daily meditation practice. But the images only grow worse. This time my body gives an involuntary jump. Briefly, I wonder if this is madness. But no. However real they seem, I know these images to be fiction not fact.

Heart racing, I try once more to meditate. True, life is tough right now. True, I'm newly arrived in a strange town, nursing a broken heart and as yet out of work. And yes, I can expect my meditation to reflect life's challenges. But isn't meditation supposed to help? Shouldn't my practice sustain me when I need it most? Another gruesome scene stampedes through me. I shift, open my eyes and start to cry. Something is wrong. After all this time, I have to ask myself: is meditation working? Despite decades of practice, the only wisdom I can summon is the wisdom to stop.

And now, twenty years on, here I am again, meditating. This time, I'm sitting with a scattering of other meditators wrapped in hats, coats and blankets in a low room with large windows. Beyond the pristine panes, there's nothing but a dim blur of forest, swallowed by swirling fog. Since yesterday when we arrived, everything has been shrouded in cloud. But as I open half an eye, I see that the mist is clearing, and above the treeline it has cleared entirely. Excited, I scan the skyline. This is to be my first glimpse of the Himalayas! From this perishingly cold, but perfectly poised, hotel-retreat, I am waiting to see the archetypal vistas of Mount Kanchenjunga stretching before me, here at the high point of the world.

Eyes wide, I peer up. But where are they? I see only a lumpy grey mountainous mass. My heart sinks at the ordinariness of it all. True, the sky above is vast and indigo, and spiked with startling white cirrus – but where are the longed-for peaks? Worried now, I tilt my head higher and a little to one side. Then it strikes me. Those delicate cloud etchings on their silk-blue coverlet, they cannot be clouds after all. Soaring higher than I ever believed possible, and disconnected from mere earth, these are the icy summits. Their tips spring up from open space itself. By some Himalayan conjuring trick, the mountains lie higher than the sky!

This, in a way, is a perfect metaphor for my journey. I have come to Kalimpong, Northern India, to meditate for a fortnight, and it's been a long road. The venture started way back after my meditation 'crashed' so spectacularly. I would have given up, but (for some strange and gritty reason) I still loved meditating. Simply, I argued, there must be something – some vital thing – I needed to learn. But like the Himalayan foothills on this first day of my retreat, the way ahead was clouded with foggy confusion. Still, I needed to know why meditation was causing me such distress. Was it my own unprocessed past coming to haunt me? Was there trauma buried deep in my bones? But if so, why wasn't meditation helping to heal? If anything, it was making things worse.

Slowly, over the following years, I began to see that the problem lay in the *way* I was meditating. Yes, at times I could sit down and create a calm space. But then startling images would come, telling me I was far from fine. My body-and-mind was not, after all, a safe, inviting place to rest. Unwittingly, what had built up inside me was an *unsafe* environment. I came to see that – as I meditated – I was also shutting out aspects of myself, parts of me that longed for expression and freedom. I was limiting myself, not expanding. This meant I must throw away the hidden rule books I had accumulated over time. I would have to start afresh. Instead of running my meditation, could I allow my meditation to 'run' me? What about complete inner freedom, with all its attendant chaos? How would it be to embrace all the things that traditional meditation seems to dismiss?

In the end, my explorations led me to a radical change in perspective – just like the one at the start of my retreat as I tilted my head to one side and discovered the Himalayan peaks. Perhaps what I sought had been there all along, but so misplaced that I couldn't see it. A subtle sliding, a gentle body-shift, and my inner world would change forever; just like my limited conception of space and the ordering of elements – is it rock and sky, or sky and rock? – that was turned on its head that day.

In Kalimpong, my *Gentle Guide to Meditation* stirred into life. It comes from the practice of 'Recollective Awareness' (page 112), the mindful habit of pondering *after* a meditation. And as I ponder, I write. Sitting on, pencil in hand, I scribble and dabble. I muse in a lazy, sidelong fashion. More often than not, I choose poetry, that pithy pathway to the deep. Following its unique logic, I have some hope of surveying the muddled and murky mind-ways through which I paddle, plunge, surf and stew as I journey within. So the poems spring directly from the source. Composed immediately after (sometimes within) my meditation, each one has helped me explore an inner landscape and discover some meaning – however momentary, dim or dusty.

In this way, the poems also affirm that – in the art of meditation, at least – our surest guide is always and only ourselves. No-one but ourselves can know the terrain so clearly, listen so long to the battles and the heartache, rejoice so fully in a life lived truly as it is, if only for a second or two.

Poems have their own footfall. Sharing them here with you, along with ideas on how to meditate, I hope this volume will inspire you to inspire yourself – to travel safely, freely and joyfully into the mystery that is you; to be ever more fascinated by your own journeys to the deep.

Setting out

Come to the beach,

Here, with me now
    beside the ocean of ordinariness.

The roar and tumble,
    the gentle lapping
        of everyday;

Let's see what the tide brings in.

I
Setting Out

Meditation is the turning of yourself within, and the discovery of what you find there when you do. Most of us have a sense of it long before we set out to learn it. If you have ever gazed dreamily out of a window, breathed in a luminous sunset, or grown still at the sound of birdsong, you already know a kind of meditating.

If you want to explore meditation further, you might allocate special time to practise it. When I am on retreat, I turn off the clocks and cover up digital time signals with sticky notes. But in daily life, you can simply set aside some minutes – as long or short you wish – which you mark as *yours*.

You can put aside what catches your attention from without, such as alluring technology. You may even choose silence over meditative music or recordings. It helps to sit quietly with yourself or others, away from the clutter of jobs and conversations.

You can never stop life flowing towards you, nor would you really want to. But as much as possible, you make this time your own.

Today we learn to fly

Today we learn to fly
Using the wings you have
Brought along, the ones
You made in school that time
With the fair-haired teacher who
Tried so hard, but probably
Cried in the staffroom afterwards.
And surprise, surprise, the wings
Never really worked.
So you added bits here and there
Over the years, always hoping
They might come good;
Hoping for lift-off.
So these are the wings we will use
Because they are
The ones you have.
And we will start
By noticing they are there.

For many of us, the first challenge is the most prosaic: *How can I find time to meditate?* Just sitting still and undisturbed may be a monumental achievement. To find that your mind still buzzes with the mundane busyness of life, it's tempting to think, *I'm no good at this!*

But learning to meditate is a journey, one in which we never really 'arrive'. Learning to meditate means learning to love ourselves as we are. And that is something we do forever because we are infinite, and because loving ourselves inevitably means loving others – and they are infinite too (and in the end, the same thing).

So, you don't need to be 'good' at meditation to take it up, or to feel the deep nourishment it can bring to your days. All of that will grow in time. What you need, over and over again, is simply to start from where you are. If you can do that, with just a fraction of curiosity and a small dose of wonder here and there, then that's enough.

For now

Don't wish for your mind
to be different from how it is;
Water does not boil faster
for glaring at it.
Things take their own time,
and you, too, are subject to
the laws of change.
You can only dip your toes
into the occasional puddles of calm
that collect in the dips and hollows
of your undulating thoughts.
Although a tiny droplet of peace
is all you find, still treasure it;
It is yours, and all you have –
for now.

To start, see how you wish to place your body. You can ask your body what it wants: *Do I wish to sit – or lie down – or stand? Can I rest this way for as long as I wish to meditate?*

It's good to be comfortable so that your body can relax. Then, however frantic you feel within, your body slows and settles without. This in itself offers calm.

At the same time, your aliveness and strength will sustain you. If you are sitting, you may decide to sit upright rather than leaning back in the chair. If you lie on your back with legs stretched out, you may decide to bend your knees up towards the ceiling. You choose positions that feel more 'awake'.

Whether you set up to be more alert or more restful, the important thing is to choose – and to choose consciously:

> *Am I comfortable enough?*
> *Does my body know I am doing something different?*
> *Have I decided to meditate?*

The way I sit

The way a frog
feels water
through its feet.

The way a leaf floats
or falls, never
in a straight line.

The way a bird's wing
unfolds into space
the colour of sky.

The way I sit,
knowing and not-knowing,
still –

Content with this.

When you sit to meditate, it's good to start without really starting. You take your time. You make space to settle. You catch up with the serene truth of existence, of being alive right now.

You may feel the weight of your body on the chair, the touch of your hands on your lap. There are your feet on the earth. Here, perhaps, are fine movements as your breath flows in and out.

If your eyes prefer to close, let them. If not, they may stay half-open, or softly-focused, drinking in your surroundings.

You feel the air against your skin.

You let your body support you.

Droplets of enjoyment

Droplets of enjoyment form
Like dew on an autumn twig,
Until the tree which is myself
Feels the stirrings of spring.

When you begin in this easy way, still and rooted on the ground, meditation often arrives by itself. Your awareness naturally expands. And when you are aware, you have choices.

If you wish, you can widen out into a broader sense of 'me'. It may come as a whole-body feeling; or perhaps as a knowing, however vague: *Here I am. This is me.*

If you prefer, you can turn towards the thoughts and feelings that come crowding in, calling for your care. Noticing them gently, with awareness, may bring relief.

You might simply step back and acknowledge it all: *This is what's here … all this; just as it is, right now.*

As we sit

As we sit, the moon rises
And mist covers the mountains;
Just one pale cloud
Rimmed with pink
Rises above the world.

You might choose to linger here or there, wherever your awareness takes you. You rest lightly in yourself. This brings discoveries.

You may find yourself drawn into your body where you discover a whole world of sensation. Perhaps your toes are tingling, or your hands feel cool against your skin, or there's a light breeze that sends a single hair to tickle the back of your neck. You may feel your breathing, too: soft, natural movements of repose and response as the air slides in and out. You may dance to the beat of your heart, feeling the pulse of your existence. These are kernels of sentience.

Suddenly, springing up from nowhere, comes a sneeze. Your nose twitches as the sneeze builds. It's a big one. Do you let it happen, that violent explosion? Or do you hold it in? This all-absorbing question may ambush your meditation entirely.

Then, that hair tickling your neck turns into a ferocious itch, and your attention is hijacked by a desperate desire to brush it away. Do you brush, or do you greet your desperate desire with love? It is up to you. Stillness, you see, has its own excitements.

However it is, your body is alive. It's a place to come home to. And the best time to be in your body is when you find yourself there anyway.

Blessings today

My blessings today
are no blessings,
my body stillness
is no stillness,
my turning thoughts
without face or name;
yet I sit and count the seconds
between one breath and the next,
and count the time
a blessing all the same.

In meditation, there are many things you can 'do' that help you to 'be'. Just sitting still and silent is one of those. This is not a stale or sorry silence, felt in isolation. Here is stillness that welcomes life. It is stillness that brims with the smells and sounds of your world.

You don't need to shut out the noises, either. Met by your easy silence, you may find 'noises' transmuting (to your ears) into simple 'sounds'. You may discover new sounds, too; sounds that lap around you as you sit at the centre of your unique soundscape.

Heard in this way, sounds within the stillness change. They collect calm. You might close your eyes and sense into space, letting your awareness ripple around you, circling just as far as you wish it to go. Here, the world comes and goes of its own accord. Textured vibrations long or short – you don't need to go looking for them. They come to you gratis. You can rest in their coming and going, the sweet simplicity of letting it happen. The world becomes your personal orchestra, a band conjured up for your very own satisfaction and support.

There's nothing you need to do – just be.

Old bones

Every morning I dig out
the pile of old bones
that the night deposited here,
here in my heart.

I see their soft indentations
imprinted in fleshy hollows.
I run my fingers down runnels and troughs,
red and sore.

I live again their quickness and their life
and sense how feelings melt their
way to freedom and trickle into day;
I listen to the man who hawks beside the river
his blanket grey like morning, who
laughs in the face of dawn.

I bend, scoop up my welling heart
into my precious fist.
I sing the world.
I sing myself into being.

Another way to feel the world's support is to rediscover gravity. It is the universal law sensed from within. An apple falling from the tree knows it as well as you: the lure of earth.

Meditation is all about earth. Earth is a place to stand, yes, but also a place of deep belonging. It is a place of connection felt deep within your bones. This coming down to earth is a practice. Time and again, you feel the weight of your body dropping down into your pelvis, legs and feet and flowing through the floor. You let everything sink and settle.

You can ask yourself: *How do I feel the ground? How do I know it's there?* Then you scan your body, waiting for answers. Or you ask: *Where do I feel supported right now? Where do I sense gravity?* Now is the time to take in – for example – the satisfying solidity of the chair, the weight of your buttocks beneath you. You sense the substance of yourself, your sheer materiality.

And why not check out your feet? See how much they know! Through socks and shoes and carpets, in high buildings, on floors suspended in space – your feet still know where safety lies, and are ready to carry you there. Sensing through your feet is another way to feel grounded. For some, it's the simplest opening into awareness:

I feel the earth – therefore, I am.

Keep consulting life

Keep consulting life.
Sometimes you can melt
and make hard edges smooth,
over and over returning to the place
where hope fell, and tarmac forsook
the greeny paths of spring.

Sometimes, there's nothing left to do
but dig for life itself, through the
blood-filled seedpods of your body;
to dig for life itself,
deep in the earth of your body,
fed and watered, oh
and stoked by stars.

The truth is, awareness changes everything.

You might try this, right now. Take your attention into your feet, and see what happens. Then, for a change, take it into your hands; or, to be really precise, into just one hand. Then wait.

If you need to wriggle toes and fingers, feel free. Here's a great reminder that your hands and feet belong to you. But when you have stopped the wriggling and they are still, when you close your eyes or look away – how do you know your hand is there? Are you sure? And are you sure it is yours? How do you truly *know*?

You may just have a general sense: *Yes, it's here and it's mine*. Perhaps you detect a pulsing, a warmth, a freshness. Or you feel your blood flow with a secret tingling. The more, the better. Let it tingle, let it flow!

This proves a special skill. It is an ancient body wisdom to sense from within. You verify your existence. You swear by your own atoms. Grounded and secure, you fill out your body.

Sensing your body from within is another way to 'be'.

Unexpected harvest

Sometimes you reap what you sow,
Only to discover a surprise harvest
Of gold and sunshine;
You sit, filled with the
Unexpected bounty of your body,
And slowly catch up with the
Tender truth of happiness.

The art of Being may be enhanced by stillness, but it is not the same as stillness. You can also meditate in movement.[1]

Closing your eyes, you will know without looking where your hand lies in space; and it knows too. It knows its own distance from your body. It senses objects nearby. If you wave your hand through the air, you will feel its arc. If you are lucky, you can touch your nose with your finger – and not miss by too much. All this is a fine art. But is it as fine as dancing? Moving through space – and knowing where you are as you do so – is a delight many of us take for granted.

To sense your body moving is another way to be mindful. You can relish movement as you move. Gently, you slide through space. Even sitting still, your body makes a hundred subtle movements, ones you can feel and follow. Movement magnifies the power of presence. It's another way to feel alive in the moment. And where movement leads, grace follows.

---

1 The technical term for sensing your body from within is *interoception*. The term for sensing your body as it moves in space is *proprioception*. Both are vital to healthy functions of body, mind and emotion.

Air

We sigh within, as the wind soughs without,
Through this glinting window on to early autumn,
Changes stir the moving air, sweeping us before;
We breathe in elemental harmony, which
Lifts us up and sets us down, right here.

Another key to aliveness (quite literally) is your breath. You may rest there naturally when you meditate, feeling the sweet-and-easy sensations of breathing. Here, every exhalation is a home-coming, returning you over and again to a state you know by heart. Here, you may find yourself 'being breathed' by your expert body. The delicious familiarity of breathing, its cosy comfort, its tides, its consonance and rhyme; however it may be – this is for you to feel, to sense, to know uniquely as only you can.

But if breathing consciously causes strain (as it does for many), then you might keep your attention light or focus elsewhere. As you relax, your breathing will regulate by itself: no need to alter it, or even notice it. Certainly, no need to criticise. A deeper sigh may show your body calming; softer breathing shows your body at rest. But that will happen of its own accord, given the right conditions for you. Focusing on the breath is not restful for everyone all the time.

Still, breathing keeps you alive – and this by itself may feel good. With every in-breath comes a slight influx of energy; with every slow and gentle out-breath, a natural calming. Befriending the out-breath may bring added pleasure to your breathing. You can luxuriate there. At the end of each out-breath is a pause, another place to rest, to revel in silence.

With no effort or intention of your own, the miracle of your body brings life, and lets it go again.

Last breath, with Bach

You flew away as if your life was merely held
By the simple tugging of a kite-string, gently
In the fingers of my hand.
And so I felt you slip into the air,
Returning to your native place
Like light back to its source,
Sliding still and silent
Into dark, soft as the womb,
The dark before creation, the dark before the dawn;
A sweet release, and swift, as resting in the
Sanctus, your spirit knew: this is the way to go.
How music was your resting place and home,
And at the last your carriage too;
How music's glorious mystery lifted you away
Beyond your outworn flesh and bone
Toward your final breath, not needed now,
For you had flown.

Now you know how much you can 'do' to help you 'be', it may be better to do nothing at all. Perhaps the most relaxing thing is to let things take their course. Perhaps it's time for time off?

So be prepared to put aside any idea of what it is to meditate. Yes, your mind may slither and slide, or hop and pop, or drift and dream. You can let it do its own thing. How is this 'meditation'? By choosing. By allowing whatever passes through. By saying 'yes' to what comes.

There is no one thing you should (or should not) do right now. In this way, *you can never fail at meditation*. There are no rules.

Meditation is an everlasting invitation to 'be', just as you are right now, whatever's happening – or not.

Summer rain

Poetry not meditation
Fills my mind,
While my body brims
With wordless energy;
I sit on with nothing to say,
As happy as a blade of grass
In summer rain.

Above all – and especially if times are tough – it's good to be kindly. Then, however rough the contents of your mind, however sore your heart, you will add a drop of kindness to your world.

With kindness it doesn't matter what you do in your meditation or what happens of its own accord. Your thoughts may come and go, like the coming and going of sea waves. You may ponder what you find, musing to your heart's content. You may sit and listen, within and without, as you would to the sound of the ocean. You may let it all wash over you and through you.

However it is, you open up your depths.

You take a journey within.

Open

How it is to feel
Entirely open,
Unconcerned and shining,
Like a mirror newly polished
Beneath a clear blue sky.

II
Curiosity and Enjoyment

Your body – your being as a whole – has its own wisdom. Winds may stir up the surface of the sea, but you are more than that. You are the whole ocean.

If there is one thing your body-and-being deeply knows, away from the surface splashing of your mind, it is how to feel pleasure. It knows how to enjoy, and so to be content, comfortable, calm.

You may dip naturally into this body-wisdom when you meditate. Or perhaps, for you, the body is a place of anxiety or pain and you will need to re-learn what your ocean-being already knows.

Still, if you are curious, you become interested. With interest, you become engaged. And it is this engagement in your meditation that will, in the end, open your body-and-self to pleasure. Curiosity and enjoyment are things to learn in meditation – and they go hand in hand.

Coral waters

Slip away from the rocks
Into orange water,
Where the sun rises
From within,
And jagged thoughts
Turn to rose-hued coral
Before your very eyes.

What helps you engage in meditation? You look for flow.

Curiosity is a current. The stronger your curiosity, the more you flow. Curious, you never lack company. You are never too far from joy, nor too afraid of sorrow. But curiosity does not come ready-made. If you feel confused, frustrated or bored, it's good to remember where your feelings reside: *within*.

Feelings live and breathe inside you. They may be felt-and-sensed in or around your body, perhaps as sensations within your torso, or in some indefinable place within. Sometimes feelings dwell mysteriously in your being, more as a 'knowing' than a 'place'. It is this body-knowing that brings you home to yourself. However you feel them, the aim in meditation is to greet your feelings with the open wonder of an adventurer.

For example, can you be curious about feelings of confusion? If so, it is likely you are no longer completely confused. Could you be fascinated by frustration? Then I suspect you are not wholly frustrated. Could you befriend boredom? Seams of kindness will modulate grey monotony.

Curiosity is the first step to enjoying what you find. Then – if only for a moment here or there – you enter the stream.

Meditation slot machine

You slot your allotted minutes
into the slot machine
of your meditation,

And wait for the fruits to line up
and shower you with gold;

You growl at the duds,
those wasted minutes
when the slot-machine's against you,
when luck won't play;

This takes you nowhere,
don't you see?
Luck is always with you,
and everything is gold.

You'll get the knack,
– I promise.

In meditation there is infinite freedom. But – curiously perhaps – it is possible to lose your freedom and limit yourself.

So, here's a question: *What are the results of my meditation?* Not the results yesterday, or in ten years' time – but here and now. If you feel limited or trapped as you meditate, if you feel like you fail, then however good the instructions, however perfect the teaching, you may decide to take stock.

Finding yourself in conflict, distant or dislodged (and I am all of these in the next poem), you might ask: *What is the flavour of my meditation today? What is its atmosphere?* If it's difficult, dull or drear, then it's time to reflect. You may wonder: *Am I choosing what I do, fully and wholeheartedly? Am I giving myself enough freedom – in meditation, as in life?*

If you are not, your body and mind will rebel.

Wrung out in Cambridge

After the fury of hours, I see
how flat the college lawn lies,
as heavy rollers turn mud-
inspired grass into college art;
as college diners descend,
pristine as napkins in their glasses,
as measured spoons and buttery sheen of knives,
penitent under strict examination
by seventeenth-century eyes
that fix from heads ruff-rimmed,
starch-sure and vexed
to bear (more than most)
their arduous history
from one dinner to the next.

So I see the shrinking centuries eked out
amongst the crinkling costumes of the past,
heads pre-severed by floating clouds of lace;
I feel the separateness of one effort from another,
yet I endorse art, such as it is.

Yes, I support nature too.
I applaud it wholly.
From a place elsewhere, I attend an after-
dinner overture to humanity;
from a seat far, far up in the gods, and a mile
from the singing star on her
operatic stage of sky,
I conduct the encore of myself.

Yes, now it's over, I consent to laze and lie,
to assume I am alive; to whisper – All is well,

As in a postcard from a distant hotel,
which may never quite arrive.

In meditation, freedom means the freedom to choose – and the freedom to let things be. This freedom comes afresh every time you are aware. Over and again, you choose what you wish to do with this moment.

Sometimes you may choose to rest on forms and structures. If you enjoy following the breath, or focusing on the body or reciting certain words – then these create a foundation. They settle and calm you, give you space to feel fully alive. Just as a river bank allows the river waters to flow, they create conditions for your mind-and-body to feel free.

There is no 'one' way to meditate, and no 'right' way either. Sometimes, you may find it more nourishing to let the mind run, or to enjoy feeling dreamy or sleepy. Sometimes, freedom means stepping back and allowing the mind-and-body to choose where it goes. Your mind needs the right to roam.

Creating conditions

If you want birds
in your garden in spring,
  buy bird seed,
    make a bird table.

If you want
your heart to open,
  relax your mind;
  make peace with your
    thoughts.

If you don't enjoy your meditation, you could check out your expectations. Unwitting 'oughts' or 'shoulds' slip in so craftily: *I should be better at this! I should do it for longer! If only I did it properly!* Perhaps you have introduced an ancient rule-book full of forgotten judgements?

If you believe such judgements to be true, they will rob you of life and joy. Deep views like these can be hard to spot. You may have an inkling only when you spy them lurking in the background of your meditation, a distant discomfort. This is the time to ask: *Is my meditation one more thing that 'I must do' – that I 'have to fit in'? Do I feel guilty when I don't meditate? Have my efforts become a chore?*

You may have heard there is a certain way to meditate or an ideal state to achieve. Understandably, you want to get things right. To put down your valued rule-book, or to question treasured expectations – this is an act of courage. To sink into your meditation as you find it – this is an act of pure possibility.

My thoughts like crows

Today, my thoughts remind me
of carrion crows, disturbing the peace
with harsh caws, with beaks
that tear into the flesh of a dead fox
the way that life tears into me.

But then I remember their black-
sheened fellowship, as they
strut along the rooftop
beyond my bedroom, as a child;
their strange sure patterning
in twos and threes
tell of hidden ways;
an animal wisdom,
I can never know.

And now, I'm strutting idly myself
off to the pet shop for puppy chews,
planning today's excursion into
the world of ordinary joy.

And I marvel to discover,
as I sit some moments more,
a stream of preciousness
that flows unbidden,
and delights me,
just because it's there.

When you sit down to keep yourself company, you might pose this question: *How can I make my time most enjoyable? What can I do to make my meditation …* ***delicious****?*

When my meditation runs out of steam – as of course it does – I lower my sights. I expect less. I lighten my touch. I remember this is nothing new: my mind is not the first to wander off, to do its own thing; I am not the first to struggle with my wayward thoughts and feelings.

Waiting for magic

I know that magic is always here,
Waiting to appear,
Utterly un-elusive.

While I do a great job
Of eluding it.

– You have to laugh.

When you meditate with curiosity as your guide, everything that comes along is part of your meditation. Under the loving lens of your curiosity, nothing is 'wrong', nothing has 'failed' – it simply looks *curious*. It's 'what is here'; here to be acknowledged, here to greet as you say 'hello'.

Whatever you do when you sit to meditate **is** your meditation – however that is for you right now.

Soul waters

Standing barefoot in the cooling waters
of my soul, tangled like lost twigs in
tumbled thoughts, all I can do is see
the meaning each one holds; each with its own
peculiar patterning, its personal delivery –

here, beneath the thought-stream,
in the current of being; deep, mysterious,
and in the end a private paradise, which
words cannot quite capture;
each arriving ripe and perfect in the
dappled light. My tingling feet press
firm against the pebbles, I bend,
collect them sweetly dripping,
feel their form, and let them go;

Back towards the charmed soul-
stream where feelings form and flow;
toward dream-currents, tending
(as they do) to health and healing,
to heaven, and to rapture too.

To look at it another way, your inner world is like a house.

This is how Rumi sees it, poet and Sufi mystic from thirteenth-century Persia: *'This being human is a guesthouse'*. His words, fragrant with freedom, offer an escape from the embroiling contents of your mind. However dark the thoughts – be it depression, meanness, malice – they can be seen in a different light. Embracing Rumi's notion of a 'guesthouse' turns your dark thoughts into 'visitors'; the same as any fleeting moment, the same as joy itself. The aim is to recognise your inner visitors – and to greet them as such: *'Meet them at the door laughing'* (Rumi tell us), *'and invite them in'*.

In the end, the journey of your meditation takes you back to your own front door. Here, even direst failure is just another caller; another aspect of yourself to welcome with love and care. Following Rumi, everything inside you has worth. Every speck of experience has value, because *'each has been sent as a guide from beyond'*.[1]

---

1 For any meditator, Rumi's beautiful poem 'The Guest House' is a gift. You will find this and other poems in *The Essential Rumi* (HarperCollins, 1997) with Coleman Barks's translations. 'The Guest House' is also available online.

All I have[1]

Mount Kanchenjunga has tresses
Of silken gold;

Lama Yuru sits in
Royal ease;

King Jambhala's mongoose lays
Gem-eggs and jewels.

Me? I've an inch of trust
And an ounce of joy.

It's enough.

---

1 'Kanchenjunga' (Khangchendzonga) is the third highest Himalayan mountain. Lama Yuru is a neighbouring peak, named for its shape (like a seated lama wearing his typical hat). King Jambhala is a protector-god of the Himalayas associated with abundance.

Another way to see it is this: you meditate as you can, 'not as you can't'. That means finding ways to make the time your own, to draw yourself in. Never mind 'success'. If your mind or heart won't settle and you can't focus on anything, you can turn instead to your attitudes. You can be curious.

In my meditation, I seek it out. I search for something – anything – to catch my interest. Even a powerful dullness of mind may serve as a place to rest and rejuvenate.

'You meditate as you can, not as you can't.'[1]

---

1 This quotation comes from a conversation with Rowan Williams (2019) in which he cited Abbot John Chapman (1865–1933): '*Pray as you can, and do not try to pray as you can't.*' From: John Chapman, *Spiritual Letters* (London: Continuum, [1935] 2003), p.109.

Old oil painting

Meditation today,
like an old oil painting of sea and storm and snow, so
blackened with age how could anyone know
where waves or winds or boats begin?
You strain and search through faint flecks of foam
the splintered shafts and tattered sails,
a broken moon, a point of light,
a contract to illuminate, just once, this restless
heaving mass, so stuck beneath its oily canvas,
rolling on unseen;
so badly in need of restoration.

Anything at all will do to catch your interest and draw yourself in. A ceaseless voice in your head playing on and on may not seem much. Still, you can pause and ask: *What does it hold of interest or of note?*

The tiniest oddity, the flicker of memory, a flash of an image – these are the tools of your trade: *Is anything happening I did not expect? Is there a dash of unpredictability?*

The unexpected

A single radio station
chatters on,
as if a single voice
balances on a single rock
in a solitary desert
that slowly comes to life
around and around
enveloping everything in a dusky haze
with its own peculiar charm –
and convincing, finally,
even the radio to try something new.

You might see it now, twiddling
its thumbs,
doing headstands,
sprouting cacti;
or spinning off to another planet
to chatter there, incorrigibly,
for its own
singular
amusement.

Sleepy meditations are especially useful because they may still hold last night's dreams. You might not find a whole dream waiting for you there. But watch out for dream fragments. Here are gifts for the curious.

A moment of wonder can lift your energy. If something entrances you even for a second or two, that's enough.

Unguarded treasure

What draws us in
from the crowded streets
of our mind,

We only know when it comes to us
fresh, unasked:

The tip of a wing,
a goshawk's perhaps,
those few feathers,
then gone;
a face half-familiar;
a wash of blue, which
softens and seeps through;
an embrace,
a sense, no more;
a lacing of hazelnuts
stitched to a bough.

Such humble intimations
from another place –
Don't look away!
These threads that draw us in
are map and measure both,
are lures to loveliness;

Fascinating steps, O meditator,
to unguarded treasure.

If you find yourself lost in pleasant plans or fantasies, why dismiss them as daydreaming? They may hold more than you know.

One morning, as I sat to meditate, I saw a beautiful sunrise before I closed my eyes. Although the meditation itself seemed to go nowhere, the memory drifted back to me at odd moments, creating islands of enjoyment amidst my tumbling thoughts. Afterwards, those islands became a poem.

So, allow yourself to dwell in a juicy plan or memory. Discover the feelings it evokes, especially the feeling as it is held in your body or being (if this is comfortable for you). Luxuriate. Savour the sensations.

This is not indulgence. It is a special skill needed in meditation: one that builds your capacity to feel what needs to be felt. It is worth practising, too, as it is a skill you will need for facing discomfort or difficulty.[1]

---

1 'Difficulty and Discomfort' is a chapter in the next meditation guide: *Into the Flow: A Gentle Guide to Meditation* (Volume II).

Morning sunrise

A luminous sunrise of red and gold
Reflecting from the ripples of the Cam;
Driven by day, and watching it unfold,
My restless thoughts that skitter on and on;
There's nothing in this stream of thinking draws
Me, tempts me into mystery, offers peace,
That leads me onwards, lifting me towards
A place of quiet, where troubled thoughts all cease;
But with the turning of my mind within,
A gentle thing, no grand or special skill,
Like a greeting, or a chance remembering,
I find the sunrise lingers in me still:
  Dawn's glorious colour that my body feels,
  Touching me softly as it bathes and heals.

You can make your thoughts useful in meditation. Thinking often holds unplumbed interest. Swept up by a tide of mental activity, you can pause and ask: *What is this like?*

Wondering '*What it's like*' may lead you somewhere – somewhere different. You may start to see associations between one thought and the next, or between one experience and another. You can consider: *What about their mood or their atmosphere? Do they have a texture or a colour?*

Asking '*What is it like*' sometimes reveals the energy of a thought. Energy, in turn, can form a mirror for your feelings: *What sort of energy does my thinking hold? What do these thoughts want me to* ***feel****?* It is when you discover their hidden feelings that thoughts generally start to settle, and something shifts.

A sense of humour will serve you well, too. As you meditate, try teasing yourself. Or riff on a theme, such as – *What's on the menu today?*

Meditation Café

What flavour shall we make your thoughts today, sir?
These delicacies we serve are for the discerning few;
Draw up a stool, sir; please, peruse the menu.

Many people start with something juicy,
A steaming slice of grudge, you say, seasoned well with fury?
Ripe resentments too, left to stew in an old pot,
We serve them on a tender bed of hurt, fresh-cut.

What next? A platter, perhaps, of pickled plans,
Eaten raw, prepared by our own hands.
This all goes down quite nicely with
A dainty dish of dreams, cooked up with
Saucy self-created scenes.

Or if it's futile fantasies you crave
Then add a dash of loneliness or fear
(Or both, if you feel brave).

Now then, you'll want dessert, let's see,
You're tempted by the film you saw last night?
Inspired choice! Scrumptious actors, I agree.
A heavenly holiday is also worth the time;
The way your puppy wags its tail (a small delight,
But equally divine). And after such a feast
You'll wash it down with slugs
Of sleepiness? Ah yes, it's true,
This is our very choicest brew.

You'll come again, I hope, where else would you go?
We're here to nourish you, and help you grow.
And if next time you find the café heaving
At least you know the menu now,
And can digest its meaning.

The question *What is this like?* leads naturally to another question: *Where is this? Where do I feel it, from within?*

A thought, a feeling, an image – experiment by tracing them even further within your body-or-being. Perhaps they can be felt in some peculiar place. It might take time to embody or describe:

Oh, just some weird-longing-bursting-bubbly feeling in my stomach …

Whale in my belly

I wish I had a whale
in my belly,
like Jonah in reverse,

Then I would know my hugeness
for what it is;
I would revel in the giganticness
of my self.

I wish I had a whale
in my belly,
like a circus wonder;

It would splash and somersault
right through me
sending me sky-high,
like a popcorn on the tip
of a waterspout.
(The crowds would love it.)

I wish I had a whale
in my belly,
it would sing me to sleep
with low, mysterious tones,
and send me dreams of vastness
and glimpses of the deep.

Affectionately, you can poke fun at your mind as it drags you along by the scruff of your awareness.

Mondays

thoughts about Mondays:
    firstly
        they should not really happen, not at all,
but if they do,
    should start with a thrush singing
    on the topmost branch
        and then carry on in such a way
that you don't notice
        mail   on the mat
or that   the porridge has   burnt
        or that   it's Tuesday, actually
    and   you've   just
                            lost   count

Even if you have no words to describe what you feel, or what is happening inside, it's good to know: *Yes. I feel it. It's here somewhere.*

This is spice for curiosity – because what is felt is real. It is the ground on which you stand in the confusion of consciousness.

So, pause to take in the enigma. You may need to give yourself 'a nothingy space' before it can be felt clearly and (perhaps) in one place.

If the feeling still evades you, maybe this is because there is no single feeling? Or no place for it? It just 'is'. It may simply feel like, '*Me – all over*'.

Then: *How is this 'me all over'? And what is it like to be this 'me', right now?*

Cage

Here, there's a cage, metallic,
hard and cold, that glints
in my mind's eye; I see it
lodged between my shoulder blades.

And here, an ancient, tender place
where wings should be; if wings
unfurl, would fly and carry me
at will, sky-bound and earth-protected,
open through and through, into a place
where no guard's needed;
Here, to my heart at rest and still.

It is easy to be fooled by the smallness of things – how unimportant they seem. It's so hard to notice what you think is irrelevant. Even if something seems absurdly ordinary – especially then – take time to explore. Here's a chance to practise curiosity and see where it leads.

One day, I moved some bamboo poles into my garden shed. Such a small act. Yet something about the smooth, silky surface of the bamboo stayed with me for an instant as I sat to meditate. Amidst the tumble, I let myself linger there and the feeling grew (and a poem, too, with its sly double meanings).

Ode to an ordinary pole

Maypole, flagpole and ski pole,
Barge pole, bean pole and dance
pole.
Life without poles, a frigid affair;
Joyless, defeated and dull,
and travelling nowhere.

Give me instead
the smooth and slender surface,
strong to my fingers' touch,
and high for my sky-gazer's eyes,
in silent defiance of gravity,
a hymn of vertical praise,
standing in perfect poise
at the still point of the world.

North and South Poles, too;
Let's not dismiss what's ordinary,
or we lose the hidden meanings,
lustrous in snowy twilight,
which turn us on our own
peculiar axis.

Telegraph, tent and silky bamboo;
Don't let the dust of everyday
hide the full moon of ourselves
from ourselves; or the clouds,
forgetful of the stars, cast shadows
on our soul's delight. What is
ordinary
has power and purpose,
beyond imagining.

Let us trace our moment here
in mast and beam and post,
stand straight and strong, a
totem pole, perhaps, both
lean and true, of root and sky,
a pledge of sorts, a crazy toast,
a paean for best and worst,
to celebrate the mysterious
markings of life.

People and pets will feature in your meditation, of course. They are so close to hand (meet my cocker spaniel, Cherub). The antics of those you love are also metaphors for what you feel inside.

Meditating like this, you never suffer from distraction because everything that comes along is a possible source of interest, and once you are interested, enjoyment is never far away.

Puppy meditation on a ball of string

My puppy catches the ragged string-end
in her little dagger-teeth, and pulls.
Reluctantly, the tangled mass inches towards her,
each indignant tug an insult freshly felt.
But in thrall to puppy-whim, the ball complies,
uncertain of its fate. It shimmies silkily
across the floor, as if to plead its case.

Cherub, triumphant, starts to dance,
claws strumming string as tickling tabla taps
upon the wooden floor. And in her dervish twirls
the ball jumps all askew, all gnarled and snagging;
all to say, a caper is an inconvenience too great,
unravelling's a slight that only pain can cure.

But loosening's a journey, and what begins in loss
may deepen into gain. So faster now it goes,
and faster still, as if unwinding were
a notion newly born, as if it finds that
spinning, once begun,
and gathering pace,
is easy, fun.

As if what disentangles here might flow forever;
for movement has momentum past itself,
and tends to grace, to utmost beauty,
and to stillness too.

My meditation now, from tentative source,
finds threads of sensing faintly felt, as
tangled knots which patience sets to grow,
to loosen slowly as they will; to touch
a form of freedom then,
and so let go.

If nothing seems either interesting or enjoyable, don't worry. Minds in meditation are slippery. It can be hard to hold onto anything. The truth is, things take time to form. Thoughts and ideas emerge slowly in the soft light of your acceptance.

It may seem strange to do less when you want more. Yet, in meditation, this is often the way.

Often, the best you can do is wait. Then, the practice is to notice how you wait. Waiting itself becomes your point of interest, your expertise. It is where you rest your attention as you sink your being into the empty moments, infinitely curious to discover what will happen next.

Waiting

Arrived in the clearing
I wait for a sign,
Even an inkling will do.
Where to go?
How to get there?
Can I travel somewhere new
Using the same old pathways?
I don't ask for much. But my questions fall
Like wishes into a well,
And waiting itself becomes
The answer.

Waiting in this way cultivates an alluring receptivity.

It’s as if you are drawn back again and again into a place where you once glimpsed gold.

The old pocket watch

Years ago, when he knew no better, this country boy
lifted out his great-grandfather's pocket watch
from its velvet box, and played with the sunlight
glancing from the bronze, and saw the answering
of the stream, where he swung it to and fro
across the rippled waves.

Years later, he remembers the plop and splash
as it drops to the depths, waking the fat trout
on its fall, and worrying the minnow shoal
on its flickering journey.

And so the man from the country is drawn back,
time and again, to the flowing ford,
each year a little older and more stooped
with the heaviness of a heart unheard.

He plunges his whittled hands down
between the slithering rock and mottled stone
into the icy trickles. Sleeves rolled high,
he touches the stream-bed, mud-brown, miry,
and strangely warm,
while a shiver blue-blotches
his wetted arm. Blind fingers searching,
he discovers the shape of sensing,
solid and slimy, fierce and fine, by turn.

And now and then, in his quiet way,
he feels the golden touch,
and rests his hand on the curving form of
what may be that watch.
Only to lose it as it slips away, to be
lost and found like this, and found and lost,
in constant quest each day.

Even a humble intention to seek curiosity and enjoyment will do. Value these precious moments, they are all yours. Savour the fruit of your efforts. As the glimpses of interest and pleasure grow in your awareness, your meditation will change. And as your meditation changes, so do you.

Finding treasure

Between this and that
there's always a pause,
however infinitesimal,
an iota of sky in the stream
of being and becoming.

If you're lucky, it will come
flooding every cell with
liquid ease, and dropping
like grace into the mirrored
pool of your body.

Most of all, it will come
if you wait as patient as
deer in a forest clearing
awash with dappling light,
and bathed in the colour of trees.

Holding still, and hidden from sight,
your waiting will one day
bring you here, drawn
by the space between
one breath and the next;
here to the place
where blessings fall
into your outstretched hand.

Truly, your thanks will be
as wide as the arc of heaven,
and as full as the earth
on which you stand.

III
Listening Within

Waiting patiently for your inner world to settle, becoming curious and interested – all this asks for a particular meditative quality. You might call it listening. It is a gentle lingering, a tender sort of '*Umm*' as you wait for your meditation to take shape. Meditation will turn you into a good listener (or a better one still) because in meditation you listen within – which is very similar to listening without.

You cannot listen fully without loving what you hear. To hear someone truly is to love them, at least in that moment. When you listen with complete openness, without judgement, you bring the rare gift of acceptance to the one who speaks – be it another person, or to a voice within yourself. In this way, listening is not just a pathway to peace, it is peace itself.

Of course, if it were that simple, peace would be easier to find.

In some ways, listening is an art form. Yet it is extra-ordinarily ordinary, too. As one lifelong listener puts it:

> *It takes time to become a good listener, because it takes time to find out that you are good enough just as you are.*[1]

---

1 Rob Foxcroft, from his beautiful evocation of meditative listening, *Feeling Heard, Hearing Others* (Antonine Books, 2018), p.252.

In the silence

I wait until it's quiet within,
then I go listening at the door;
for it's only when the voices die,
we hear what all along they
tried to say.

And into that silence, like a song,
the music of our bones and blood,
our simple hurts and dangers,
come alive and live again;
and singing through us
make us what we are;
and in the silence play the tune
for what we may become.

But how can you listen happily if your meditation only echoes back the turmoil of your mind?

Here, you may seek a kind of listening which comes from your core, as you sense with your whole being; with body, heart and mind.

In a moment of true listening, there is no room for harsh or critical voices saying you are not good enough, or that you are flawed, or that you will never feel happy. Those voices fall silent because your mind is filled instead by your listening. It is here, in these moments of unstudied sincerity, that calm tiptoes towards you.

Meditating is all about setting the scene. Sometimes, the play of your mind will settle and give you what you hope for; but often it will simply do its own thing. So, you listen with the merest intention to be open and curious.

Knowing how extraordinarily powerful your wishes are when you feel them from within – well, that's the start of everything. The middle and the ending too.

Today's grand plan

Today I will do
all those things I have planned,
and some that I have not, too.
I'll set in train countless projects,
see countless others through:
clean the house, declutter, mend,
pay bills; start life itself afresh
because this day is new.

Because my intentions gallop before me
like horses, wayward and wild,
and I must learn to love them
in their passions,
their sincere purposes,
their flights of fancy;
and not to criticise the day,
call foul, find rods to beat myself,
to carp and cry
as a different day unfolds;

Before even breakfast beats me
to the door, before the kitchen clock
has scorched my careful list
with its withering gaze,
before the morning traffic has jilted
the waiting streets, or redundant
verbs can sneak inside the broadsheet
of my life, or the minutes
squirrel themselves away into spaces
my words have left behind.

Because while I'm busy arguing with fate,
it arrives as surely and as ill-timed
as my neighbour bearing blue eggs,
as the voice of a friend, as a broken pot
weaving its careless patterns across the
floor.

Because frustration is a wall that
I must scale to meet what's real
and right before me.

Because without doubt, when
I pause to breathe, I land
always in myself,
in this body, always
here and now.

So that by evening, wandering through
this shimmering summer's end,
led by some other strange intent,
I stand shoeless in a field
of fading hoof prints;

I lean into an illumined twilight
in deep and dusky content,
holding a single rambling rose
– perhaps the last of all –
and watch its tender petals
as they loosen and fall.

Could you imagine listening to yourself as if you were listening to a friend; a friend you have known for so long that you have made peace with their foibles; a friend who is dear, not *despite* their funny ways, but *because* of them? Listening to yourself in meditation is the same as this.

However frowningly your friend begins (seizing the wrong end of the proverbial stick, and prodding it in your direction), you just listen. Instead of fuming, you even smile. You refrain from offering your usual reasonable remarks, and you go easy on your wise suggestions – because all that would stop you hearing what your friend really wants you to know. In the end, this is how they need to say it; in their own zig-zag manner, in their fuzzy and infuriating way. Understanding this, you just listen.

To listen wisely, you give up trying to be wise.

Listening

Listening to our bodies is like
listening to people;
What's without is within,
one speaks to the other.
It's the same everywhere.
We hear ourselves
in the sky-borne cries of birds,
in the crunch and patter
of feet on steady pathways, in the
orchestral crescendo of a passing train.
We enter a new world, with no known preview,
with nothing in our luggage but love.
And everything we meet is wonder, is
entirely fresh, in constant motion.
We listen way beyond hearing,
with every body-sense and none,
to the swirling, image-rich flow,
which gathers and mingles and swells
and turns like a moving tapestry in the
woven fibres of our being.

When you listen to yourself in meditation, it helps to listen beyond words. You listen with your whole self, tinglingly present. You let yourself resonate in heart, gut, spirit or soul.

You may be sensing, rather than hearing.

You may breathe in what you hear, or lean into it, or let it flow through you.

You let all your senses come alive.

Chasing thoughts

A dog chasing a squirrel
Every which way:
The dog is fast
The squirrel faster.
Mad blur of grey,
Pelt and patter,
Bark and scurry,
Siege and stalemate
At the tree;
Like these embattled thoughts,
Hunted by circumstance,
Running scared;
What these inchoate voices know
And without words,
Tell so well.

When you listen in this way to others, you may be drawn in without trying. Nothing to add and nothing to prove. Here, your most valuable gift is sweet humility. You accept others as experts in their own worlds.

The same is true when you listen to yourself. It's like living with question marks, without seeking answers. It's about 'not knowing best'. It's giving yourself the freedom to feel what needs to be felt – felt fully, in its own way, in its own time. Your job is simply to keep yourself company. You allow your experience just as it is, accepting (if you can) that your inner world knows what it needs. You acknowledge. You say: *Hello.*

You might ask: *Does it feel alright to say 'hello'*? Or: *Is it okay to feel this?*

Or you summarise: *This is how I am right now. This is what's here.*

However you respond, the trick is not to fight what comes along unasked and unwanted. Instead, you are kind to yourself. You remember you are 'good enough' just as you are.

Listening to yourself with full-bodied wordless attention means listening without agenda. You make no attempt to change. Curiously, that's when change happens.

Listening within

When you stop and listen,
ear to the ground,
you hear the murmurings
of this earth, yes, faint at first,
as it bears witness to the
rights and wrongs of time;
where blood and battles spilled
upon the ground; where
lovers spread their tender bodies
on the sun-bleached grass;
where babies lay and sickened bodies fell,
and tears and laughter soaked into the soil.
Listen to the ground and learn its secrets well.
They speak of you, and live in you,
and ask that you, and you alone, will tell.

To listen beyond words, you listen beyond scenario or storyline. Narratives come from somewhere else, from a state-of-body as much as a state-of-mind (from one angle, body and mind are the same thing). So you don't need to disbelieve your ideas; but you don't get taken in by them too deeply. You hold firm, remembering they feed on more than fact. They are fed by feelings too.

This moves you into a deeper listening space where your thoughts carry subtle messages from the realm of feeling.

Thoughts are not the same as feelings. But they are not different either. They are a mingled expression of life. In meditation, it is good to welcome both: thoughts and feelings. You might ask again:

What is this thought wanting me to feel?

Towards the source

Thoughts are not the things
distracting you from feeling;
Thoughts are the feelings, yes,
the flower and the shoot.
And you must travel down the stem
Towards the root; and there,
and there, within the soil
you find the source.
You find what must be felt.

A planning thought may hold you in a vice-like grip for an age. Yet implied in that bored, dragging, anxious monologue – the pressure of 'getting things done' – you may find the sense of how it *will* be when they *are* done. Perhaps your planning mind is trying to tell you how good that will feel, what a relief.

You can test this out, even in the middle of a meditation. You take a planning thought as it comes along, and ask yourself: *How will I feel when this [task] is over?* You drop in the idea, much as you would plop a pebble into a pond – and watch for the ripples.

How will this feel when it is all complete, when it is all okay? You invite your body-and-being to tell you. You listen for resonance. You give the answer time to form. Deep inside, you may know the answer: *Ah, it will feel like **this** when it's done!* If you catch a flavour of this feeling, however hazy, then breathe it in deeply. Feel it as fully as you like. Bask. Enjoy!

True, the job is not yet done – but you hold it differently. The job is the same, but you are different.

New release

Day after day, the same visitor.
We sit, staring, at the barren screen,
and the emptiness it brings
lodges in a place that presses near,
but not quite inside, our hearts.

If we could tidy those unkempt moments,
where the minutes eddy in upon themselves,
and the weighted hours collapse
for want of art,
we might have something to say, some way
to recover the elemental electricity,
out beyond the camera lens
and looping replay.

We might find ourselves backed
by a whole crowd of extras,
pounding on our door and ready to enact
the first take, in the first cut
of the new release:

the indescribable story of us.

A mind of torrential planning or indecision is not, after all, a failure to find calm. Simply, there is more to be felt than you have space for.

You can test this out too – if you're feeling brave. As you meditate, ask yourself: *How would it feel for this vital thing (the one that's been plaguing me for the last three days)* ***not*** *to get done, or* ***not*** *to be resolved?* This raises the stakes. It may be unthinkable. The idea of ***not*** doing [whatever it is] may fill you with a nameless feeling of … *Eurgh!*

So perhaps *Eurgh* holds the clue? *Eurgh* could be the very thing that is driving your racing thoughts. This nameless '*Eurgh*' may be what your frantic mind wants to stop you feeling. It may be too tough for you to feel all this just now, without some support.

Thoughts often mask a sense of overwhelm. They dive in to protect you. They battle with stress, and strain for solutions. But if you could sort it all out with your mind, you would have done so already.

Something new is needed. Listening mindfully to your feelings is one way to find the support you need inside yourself.

Sea rock

We sail a long time
Before reaching the rock,
Jagged and uninviting,
Grey sea and spume, which lashes
And sucks at granite edges,
Many thousands of years until smooth.

And here we are at last,
Against the odds,
Against currents and winds
And the pain of it all;
Straining against the elements,
Forced back for hours on end, way off course,
Many thousands of minutes
Until we feel what needs to be felt,
In the ocean of our lives.

In my meditation poems, you see me struggling with a thousand thoughts, seeking in different ways to come into relationship with them.

You find me, again and again, searching below the thinking to enter deeper realms of feeling from which the thoughts have come.

Open sky

Armies of progress march
across the open skies
of my mind;

While magnitudes of orchestras
play on, that single thunderous tune
which lodged here last Tuesday
and has not stopped since;

While I have planned a thousand conversations,
lost empires and seen battles won, all in the same
cloud-monologue that built my self-made skyscape
yesterday, and the years before.

I don't know how to change.
With just these same old thoughts
I grow more the same.

And it's only with infinite patience,
with my obstinate belief in gardens
and the return of May, in water and
sun and seasons, that the
marching armies fade.

My too-familiar self will soften
the sky; to show its mystery
through the open spaces
of my mind.

Listening within is complex. Your inner world is complex. Very often there is more than one inner voice calling for attention. Recognising this means you can listen to each voice in turn. They are neither contradictory nor complicated – just different.

Something in me is 'like this,' I say.

But then again: *Something else in me is 'like that'.*

And after a while, both are there. That's just how it is:

And that's okay.

No time today (song)

ME:
I don't have time to sing today,
Important things are in the way.
I don't have time to meditate,
To cogitate,
Recuperate,
Investigate,
Or fulminate,
Interpolate,
Regurgitate,
Procrastinate,
(continue ad lib)
I don't have time, I don't have time, I don't have time;

ME (AGAIN):
And yet the river flows,
my puppy sleeps,
my breathing slows.
And swans swim on the streams
for countless years;

SWANS:
We don't have time. We don't have time.
What's time to us?
We don't count time,
We don't know how time feels.

It is good to hear every inner voice separately. Even if they are related, each belongs to a separate thread – a different feeling or state. Here, listening turns creative. You might ask:

If this feeling were a colour, what colour would it be?
If my mind were the weather, what weather would it be?

Each metaphor carries a bundle of emotions, a distinct energy, a feeling-state of mind-and-body. You might see each one as a 'visitor' in the room, each with its own distinct personality. You could ask:

What sort of character is this?

You may spend several days allowing a character to take shape, and for a name to emerge – one that fits completely. Here are some 'characters' I (and other meditators) have befriended over time:

The Waif, the Fun-Child, Armadillo, Judge Noble,
The Blind Coachman, Caged Tiger, Enchantress….

Naming affirms them as part of you, as part of life.

Lord of Life

Surprisingly sudden, the way
the clouds and sun pour,
on to your naked skin,
skilled lessons – in
cool and warm,
in go and come,
in shudder and shine –
with such bounty of shadow and shame,
of grace and liquid light.
Can you bask in both?
It asks you every time.
Ah, here's the calling;
Lord of Life! We answer
in your name.

If your feeling is too faint to name or locate, you might ask: *How do I know it is there? How do I know I am feeling this?*

Exploring in this way helps you to stay in your body for longer. You keep sensing within. Has this half-felt, hazy feeling any sort of texture or shape? Does it have edges? What's it like – *exactly*?

Don't be surprised if – as soon as you notice the feeling – it disappears. Perhaps the feeling is not ready to be felt? The very act of sensing, the simple fact of awareness, affects how and what you feel. But for as long as you are curious, you can keep tracking within:

Does this feeling grow, fade or stay the same?
Does it move around?
Or something else entirely?

Treasure hunt

Losing my trust in words,
and the infinite world
words feed on.
Losing my faith in answers,
in infinity (and beyond);
the truth that what is near
is also far, and what is small
holds meaning without measure.
Losing my anchor, and my guard
against grey tides of dullness,
and drear monotony of mind.

Life without colour is no life at all,
No living, no sensing, no ground;
What's caught in the mind
is not felt in the body –

Go, seek it there!

Listening deeply includes confusion, a willingness to be lost and startled.

If you meditate seeking clarity, you may miss much of the message.

Starling flight

If you've seen starlings
  take flight,   heard them too,
dark confusion of wings
    felt-disturbance of air,
self-created suddenness   and startle;
  knowing this, you know too
    the ways of mind,
confused patternings   and distant skies,
    pointillist scatterings   of space,
though nothing but   movement,
    fugitive,   no flow;
and it's no wonder   the tree left standing
  looks bare, laden with winter,
    the last fruit of the year, scanty hopes
of spring,   yet sap-stored
        and sure within.

It may be surprising to discover how much of you is set against listening altogether – against any kind of awareness, come to that.

Mole (1)

Deep in the tree roots of my world
Lives mole,
Snug and sleeping, cocooned
In his own warmth.
He is cushioned round by deepest moss;
No sharp twigs or scurrilous beetles
Can disturb him.

Oh, don't be fooled by the velvet fur,
Palest mauve where his barely-twitching ears
Poke modestly through his recumbent curl.
He is more solidly averse,
More rocklike and more fixed
Than you suppose.

Given his way, spring would come
Only on his terms (and often does).
And that shimmering streambed of rose-
Coloured light, with sunset glancing through
Its rippling waters, that promise of moonlight,
That augury of day — He doesn't see it.
Nor wants to.
Nor, given his way,
Ever will.

Mole (2)

Dear Mole, Lord of velvet darkness
And soft ways,
What can I give you
Before I leave for the light?
Let go your tiny clutching hands,
  Let go their autumn acorn,
  And open your sleeping nest
  To the windy night.[1]

[1] A sleeping mole, with 'hands' proportionally large to its body, is not actually hibernating. Moles do not hibernate.

Whatever comes is part of you, is held in every cell of your body, and needs your care. We are lucky, in this way. There's always something 'there' waiting to be loved.

David

I knew I was there, long before
the chisel found me out, before
the marble contours of my body
traced the waiting air with freshness;

while still the shreds and shards
of my birthing bleached the naked floor,
dusting the sculptor's muscled limbs,
whiting the hair on his living arms.

I know what it is to melt from stone,
to stir from shaped imaginings,
to conjure crucibles of name and form
from sunlight pooled in polished hollows;

And so it is, I wait for Michelangelo;
his touch and time, to turn
this fixity to flow.

The inner world holds many surprises. Just when you think you know how you feel (*Oh, today, I feel grisly!*) you might be surprised to find your inner world telling a different story (*How unexpectedly pleasant within!*).

No matter if it's just for a second or two. Listening to what feels good is nourishing – very nourishing. And it increases your capacity to feel the same again.

So if you feel the faint brush of beauty, or sense an instant of hidden grace, then linger as long as it lasts. Take the moment for what it is. Savour its quality, its texture. Take time to hear its history.

Collared dove

A collared dove came,
like grace, into my garden;
and a second, too.
And so, my dove-grey meditation,
a gossamer thread of stillness,
an encircling white, my companion
and mate, like the doves,
before they flew.

In meditation, you can give your mind the right to roam. This will take you on unexpected journeys through time and space. It is okay to move out of the present moment. This will happen anyway. So let it happen with awareness, with ease, with grace.

You can choose to be curious – to listen gently:

Who or what is waiting for me here today?

One day, sensing wistfulness, I let it draw me in. Following its thread, I turned time-traveller. I entered the Golden Lands. Here, in the realm of fairy magic, I encountered my childhood, and a memory of my dad – who somehow preserved his faith in fairy-tales.

So, let yourself dream and watch where it takes you.

Meditating freely, may the Unknown be your friend and guide.

Sonnet for the Golden Lands

Yes, I have wandered in the realms of gold,
Rich-garnered tales of kings with golden thrones;
Where royal princes, handsome, young and bold,
Fall under sad enchantments, cursed by crones;
How one strange tale speaks of a stolen child
Who, raised in deepest forests, learns a spell,
To conjure creatures beautiful and wild,
And share the secrets only they can tell;
Where magic weaves its ways through lands of spice,
With incantations rare in rune and rhyme,
Which summon gentle genies in a trice,
Where love and goodness triumph every time;
    These glimmering lands I lost and left behind
    Still cast their golden shadows in my mind.

THE END

And now, over to you …

Where Next?

This is the first of three volumes that move ever more deeply into the realms of meditation.

The next volume, *Into the Flow*, explores strong forces that shape our journeys to the deep. Meditation will highlight our greatest resources and reveal our greatest challenges. Often, this means other people. Starting with *Friendliness and Love*, meditation becomes an ideal place to nourish relationships. In the next chapter, we face *Difficulty and Discomfort*. How may meditation support you in these times? And why does it feel so hard to meditate, even when you know it helps? Exploring *Shifts and Transformations*, we plunge in further still. Here, subtle changes impinge and you are brushed by something new. It may be hard to see small particles of light within a dark place. But they are there. There is more to life and living than we can ever know. It is in these small moments of change that longed-for transformations emerge, and you catch them from the corner of your eye.

Series Contents

A Note on My Approaches

Many influences flow into my meditation, and into this book.

Recollective Awareness is a method of meditation that welcomes every aspect of your inner experience, including thinking. It is taught by Jason Siff in his books *Unlearning Meditation* (Shambhala, 2010), *Thoughts Are Not the Enemy* (Shambhala, 2014) and Buddhist novels. Online sites: Jason Siff and Recollective Awareness.

Focusing is a mindful gateway into the world of the 'felt sense', first formulated in the 1960s by philosopher and psychotherapist Eugene Gendlin. I recommend Eugene T. Gendlin's seminal work, *Focusing* (Bantam Books, 1st edn 1978) and Ann Weiser Cornell's *The Radical Acceptance of Everything* (Calluna Press, 2005). Online sites: The Focusing Institute and the British Focusing Association.

Somatic Experiencing, based on the work of biophysicist and psychologist Dr Peter Levine, develops the skill of felt-sensing for healing overwhelming distress and trauma. See Peter A. Levine, *Waking the Tiger* (North Atlantic Books, 1997), *Healing Trauma* (Sounds True Inc, 2008), and *In an Unspoken Voice* (North Atlantic Books, 2012). Online sites: Somatic Experiencing Association UK, Somatic Experiencing Trauma Institute.

Nonviolent Communication was developed by clinical psychologist Marshall Rosenberg in the 1970s, and is recognised internationally as a method for dealing with conflict and confrontation. See Marshall B. Rosenberg, *Nonviolent Communication: A Language of Life* (Puddledancer Press, 2003). Online sites: Center for Nonviolent Communication, UK-NVC.

Acknowledgements

With thanks to a swan on a certain day,
To Greg for getting in its way;
To Jason for the Himalayan peaks,
A place to meditate (and sometimes sleep);
To mum, hearing poems freshly brewed,
For helpful noises, love and food;
My thanks to Tony, thanks to Rowan,
For kindness and for making it happen.

My gratitude flows out to these, and all who have shared my journey to the deep. With Bevis, I began a new venture toward aliveness. In her reading of my poems, my 'Right Honourable Friend' ChuChu added an exquisite sensitivity that I am not sure they possess without her. My neighbour Susie introduced a critique of natural history metaphors and insight into the way of moles. Warm thanks flow also to 'Armadillo' Mark for being himself, to Elinor for writerly blessings, to David and Giana for valuable late changes, and to Robert for early promptings. I am unstintingly grateful for my three marvellous musketeers, Kay, Peto and Sinhaketu; and I take great pleasure in appreciating Alison for her care, Charlotte for pandemic sanity and literary laughter, James for kingly interventions, and Kath for illuminating the divine comedy of meanings. I am honoured by artist Celia Read's kind permission for her work *Big Blue*, which perfectly captures the spirit of the book, and grateful to everyone at Mud Pie for the journey onwards and mudwards. Finally, of course, deep thanks to Mike, for his stream of love and morning porridge.

Index of Poems (by first line)

Index of Poems (by title)

About the Author

Dr Elizabeth English was appointed as Cambridge University's first ever Mindfulness Practitioner. Her courses are the subject of research published in *The Lancet* showing significant benefit to students. Elizabeth draws on four decades of personal meditation practice and her ordination within a Western Buddhist tradition, as well as her doctoral research at Oxford, where she studied Buddhist meditation texts. She is also a certified teacher of Mindfulness, Focusing, Somatic Experiencing and Nonviolent Communication. She lives in Cambridge with her cocker spaniel, Cherub.

If you have enjoyed this book, and would like to order one for a friend, please scan this code:

Printed in Great Britain
by Amazon

79666470R10080